From Soul, to Mind, to Paper

Melody Crowther

BookLeaf Publishing

Presentation by *BookLeaf Publishing*

Web: www.bookleafpub.com

E-mail: info@bookleafpub.com

ISBN: 9789357692052

First edition 2022

DEDICATION

This, and every book I write hereafter, is for my school English teacher Mrs S. leHair. You don't know how much you encouraged and inspired me. Perhaps this will give you an idea.

Also, for my Auntie Louise. For everything.

Death by Candlelight

The flickering flame, so tender but bright
It is my only light for tonight.
She dances in the still air
As if breaths of whispers are encouraging her.

The lone traveller's companion
A seductive siren for the weak,
A beacon of hope for the strong.

This flame, this light, can burn down cities
She can ruin lives with just one bite.
Nobody knows where she comes from
Nobody challenges a fight.

My candle, she brings me peace
And although I am alone, someone is here
Enabling her, with otherworldly breaths, to
dance,
And to put the human eye in a hypnotic trance.

Scarlet red, blood red tower
She stands proudly while her subjects cower
Cower before her deadly reign,
This Queen who can only be defeated by rain.

Suddenly-

She spits and sputters, she trips over her feet
She reaches out for a saviour-
But I shake my head no, you cannot cheat,
And slowly her throne melts into the ground.

She spits and sputters, she begs for redemption
I focus on her light to ease the tension.
Reaching out with heavy wax arms, she cries-
She does not cry. She wants to live, not die.

She stops, suddenly-it must finally be time to
leave.
I glance at this candle, who could destroy many
And with a wink, a breath, a kiss, a blink,
I forever end her life.

Scrawlings of a Sleepless Night

Why can't I sleep?
Could it be
Memories of days long gone
Succumbed to the curse of time?

Smothering me like ocean waves
Sweet for the soul but bitter to taste.
Singing sirens dragging me down
To a place so bad yet feels so good.

Or could it be
Regrets of past and present?
Clawing at my heart, drinking my blood
Wolves under full moon's torments.

Perhaps it's the mind-consuming anxieties?
Parasitic tortures which never fail
In which never falter?
No…don't be silly.
It's that damn phone, simply.

Sensitive Souls

Desperate words fall from my mouth
A devastating avalanche of pleas.
Not excuses-just explanations;
But your defences go up and I'm forced to my
knees.

Ask me to explain, and I shall,
For I have nothing to hide.
You ask to hear, yet you do not listen,
You dash my precious words off a cliff
And let them wash away with the tide.

Salt burns on fresh wounds
I apologise, and I heal with scars.
You apologise, and I heal with tougher skin
In my dreams only-
I must not, I must not-
I must not think too fast.

Bloody-footed ballerina, star of the stage,
Put upon the public eye and she dances her
grace.
An empire built from her own calloused fingers,
Then she trips once, cue the downfall,
Of her kingdom and her throne.

I always thought,
"Do the right thing.
Make them happy, and you will not suffer."
So I did what they want, and was told,
"Grow a spine, no one will like you
They'll abuse you unless you grow tougher."

The price you pay,
The price you pay for them to let you stay.
Hearts so full of gold
But still with flesh and blood.
Broken, beaten, torn to ribbons
Stomped down, left to rot in the mud.

Lovers in the Forest

It's cold up here,
The untrained mind doth muse.
It's damp and it smells of-
Of rotting wood and dead flowerheads-
I would prefer to go home and snooze.

Hear me! I cry,
I must not lose your time!
To this forest I bring you,
So that you may see true life.

The sweet stench of nature fills the senses
The air thick with perfume after summer's first
rain.
Leaves fallen from glorious towers
Bequeathed to the earth to assist more life,
And the winding branches create a beautiful
bower.

Flowers killed by a harsh winter's battle,
But they shall bloom again,
See the afternoon sun glistening over the land,
Bringing rejuvenation at the start of winter's
end.

Hear the spirits of the woods whisper through
the trees,
Ancient kings of the Earth and Seven Seas.
Tiny dancers flit between the eyes
And we are blind, to the beauty, we are blind.

Between the eyes, between the lines,
Lie secrets of the world surrounding.
The creatures of myths, wonders of legends,
The royal towers and gateways to the heavens
How humans have not infiltrated is quite
resounding.

Branches and heartstrings snap
When wondrous trees are felled
I shall be the voice of the voiceless
Until all violence is quelled.
Bind yourself to me,
As the vines bind to the birch tree
Nature loves itself to let itself grow,
Will you love me enough to let us grow?

The little bird perched upon a stickly thornbush
Shall feast upon rubies and diamonds
And at the end of the day, in her nest she shall
rest,
Free from the land, free to the silence.

The River No Longer Smiles

The river has not smiled since the summers of
yesteryear
When the children gave it life and cared not for
smokes and beer.
Little boats would sail through and canoes
would ride the ripples
The fish would dance, and at bare skin they
would nibble.
The river was kind, and she still is-
She will never let anybody be hurt.

The children left for the battlefield,
For wars on the streets and in their own homes.
The river is left alone
Thriving on fleeting attention.
Sometimes the heartbroken ones come to her,
And they cry to her, and she cries with them.
That's why the river no longer smiles.
Although the years have torn us apart,
The river, she still has a heart.

The rooftops lost their voices while screaming to
be saved
They used to sing melodies of peace.

Harmonies of harmony, songs of lives to be
envied,
Over time, the melodies ceased.
Replaced by screams of anger,
Bellowing and fighting, endless clangour.
We may escape through the doors
But the rooftops cannot run.
They house the violence within
And keep it within their walls
Nowhere to run.

The walls watch on, as slaps are delivered
From one loving to one loved.
They watch and witness and then after,
They must look at each other
And force wretched, tinned laughter.

Smile at the river,
She craves our love.
Smile at the walls
Touch them tenderly, white dove.
Smile at the people
The bruises shall fade away
Perhaps we may live in harmony
Again, perhaps, someday.

Crippling Dreams

Do you ever dream of
A house that houses all your happiness,
Trapped in there is the ghost of yourself
But the ghost isn't really trapped, they're in
Paradise

You want to open the door
And go inside, and see love,
Smell life, and feel free,
You're welcome here
This is your home after all
But the windows are boarded up.

Time doesn't exist in there anymore
But you still run there for solitude
But the windows are boarded up
And no matter how hard you scrabble
At the harsh wooden doors
You can never get in.

Even when your fingers
Have been ground to the bone
You can taste blood, you can feel blood
In every receptor
And the windows are still boarded up

And you'll never get in
And the ghost is left alone
Thank God the ghost is happy
You sacrificed a lot for that.

Puppet Flesh

Right now, life is in a
State of decay
A chaotic circus in disarray
Nobody is trained,
And everything goes wrong all the time
And no matter how hard I try
I cannot escape the ghosts that fly
Around my spirit
But it's fine.

The water offers solitude
A place to quell my storming head
The sharp coolness of the water
Works to replenish my psyche
Move along, let me rest here on the riverbed.

I'll slip into the ocean
Glide gracefully between the salty sheets
And then I'll dance if you please,
Moving gracefully with the other dancers,
Who are here for the same reason as I;
We do not belong
To the disastrous puppet show above
With their painted marionettes
And their sly wooden movements.

The music will never stop
As long as we keep dancing
And we keep knowing
That this is where we are truly alive,
Our flesh is one with the water,
Not above with their painted marionettes
There are no strings here
No rope-masters with brass hooks
To dangle down humbling threats.

When the sun burns up and shrivels
A puny prune on a baking-tray,
When the moon disintegrates
And falls away, crumbling
Like a heart too broken to be saved,
When the ocean dries up
Taking the magic with it
And the Earth finally cracks under the pressure
Of keeping it all together in vain
We'll go the way of the waves
Sail away, not into watery graves,
We will live forever
As marks of the revolution
Legends to be whispered about
Myths to be admired.

Tell the Moon

Tell the Sun
To give me some life
Some happiness, some ease,
Perhaps even a wife.

Tell the Stars
To watch my every move
For without the light,
I have nothing to lose.

Tell the Moon
Never to waiver
Life deals her cards
She has no favour.
Tell the Moon
I have no interest to stay,
Tell the Moon
To take me away.

Emerald Valley

What words may convey the sheer beauty of the
earth?
Not all of the world is catastrophically evil-
Just a fair few of the people.
Is this all a big lesson? What do we learn?
We are so excited to leave this world behind
And experience the next life
But is that what we deserve?
Poor Mother Nature
Building herself to keep us alive
And we repay her by destroying her.
The old gods weep in despair
They have no power here,
The heathens strayed too far for redemption.

Take a walk down a valley of emeralds
Take in the sweet smell of life, dance with the
flowers,
So gentle in the breeze, and the flowers sing,
And we cannot hear it.
We are wrapped in our pods of darkness.
We can unravel, but if we keep our souls weak,
It shall soon pull us
Right back in.

Australia

Forget the lights of New York
And their statues and spires of success,
The riches dreamt of by the poorest
The hopes for everything and nothing less.

Forget the surliness of London
With their business suits and stocks,
Golden royals upon a pedestal
Over to which everyone flocks.

Forget the enchantment of France
The television romance calling,
Desperate lovers run to Paris,
Where their dark-haired conquests leave come
morning.

It's the golden rays I crave
Melting over the land
The rusty red rock of Uluru
Oh what a sight, simply grand.

The Kookaburra sits in the old gum tree
The water laps in the Harbour
The reason that this land is mine
Is thanks to my Oi, Mate! father.

One day we walked along the Harbour,

The sun bore down and I was there with my
father.
We saw two women, they were lost.
A broken-down car and their language the same,
Off they go, to help-
A few Old Mates and my father-
Off they go to help
The Asian women along the Harbour.
They gave us-
My cousin and I-
They gave us coconut ice cream
With coconut shavings and a little plastic spoon.

The golden sun bore down
On the land so rich and true.
We never saw the women again
After the men fixed their car,
The coconut ice cream trickling to our stomachs
That was thanks enough.

Through the open roads we travel,
Winding, bordered with exotic nature,
Walls of trees and leaves and cacti
In the clear night sky lies Ursa Major.
The passport I hold is post-Brexit blue
It is my most prized possession.
It has on the cover a kangaroo and emu
(Because they can't walk backwards-there's a
lesson!)

A Lover's Caress Makes It All Go Away

When his fingers draw
The map of our future
On my back
And the stars align
In his lovely green eyes,
Whirlwinds of emotion that
Only he can tame.

He does not think much of himself
But I see wonders in his soul
He's a tough one, of steel at that,
For outsiders his heart is black as coal.

Tame him like a dog,
A wild goat or centaur
Do not run, do not give up,
To me he doth implore.

"I will never do to you, what others did to me,"
At the first sign of abuse, we both know to flee.
But there shall be no fleeing, not from this love
of mine,
As a heart so golden and pure
Is so rare to find.

It matters not what is in his trousers-
Money, muscles, a ticket out of town,
Right way up or upside down,
It is deep waters that I crave,
An ocean of You, an ocean to explore,
I want to find the secrets you condemned to the
grave.

We're torn apart every day,
Torn not from each other, but from ourselves;
Our own hearts, our morals, placed precariously
Upon fragile, delicate glass shelves.
But at the end of the day
When the long light finally fades,
It is you who is there
It is you who makes it all go away.

Cigarettes After School

The slow-killing smoke
Smells like my friend's kitchen on
A Sunday morning
While the night before hands over our heads
And it is
The most comforting smell of all.

It reminds me of the days
When we'd have to hide it all
Only teachers knew the smoke could be blue
And behind the tennis sheds, we'd lie,
"Blue smoke you say? Miss, are you feeling
okay?"
We'd steal away to the forest behind the
sixth-form blocks
And to the animal care sheds
And to the green box
Thinking we needed a break from tiresome
school days.
Back then,
A pack was a fiver, if that-
But like everything else nowadays
Prices rose to disappoint.

The murderous smoke

Smells like a hug from mum
When she returned home from the rain
And a cloud of sweet perfume blends in
But if you're young enough
She'd put her clothes in the bin.
We grew up anyway
And picked up the habit too.

Cigarettes behind the English block
Keeping a sharp eye on the ticking clock
Rush to the toilets to wash our hands,
Back to class feeling grown-up and glam.
Those were the days when
We'd pay fifty pence per stick
A whole pound if we were desperate enough
The anti-smoking ads just did not click.

Cigarettes after school
Taking the long way home
Through fields with lavender bushes
Which we'd rub all over ourselves
And we'd hit a vape, too,
To get the smell off our lips,
Looking back, we thought we were so clever,
But we were stupid as shit.

sorry

by accident i
grazed your hand
ever so slightly
as you passed me something.
i said
'sorry'
but i choked
on the smoke
in my throat.
my 'sorry'
was meaningless
because it was such a minor mistake
that wasn't even a mistake at all
and
you didn't hear me anyway.

observing the town from the top of a hill

Beautifully painted canvas
A fragile phenomenon,
Interrupted by invasive metal towers
Miles and miles of powered wires
Once born, never shall they be gone.

The ocean rushing in the distance
Only in a world when I shut my eyes.
Engines polluting, deceiving, mistreating,
Core-eating, a machine's treaty
Beauty thieving.

The sky melting over the land
Turning day into night with
a lovely deep blue hue.
The lights of buildings built to destroy
Glimmer, dainty fairies, proudly,
Upon the corrupted land ocean, nightly.

Stage

The world is but a stage
Upon which fools do play
Unscripted, undirected, unnatural;
Unhinged in all ways.

I, a lowly writer,
Can script only my own life
And to my despair these fools run rampant
Blindly falling for meaningless trife.

We, the cast, we were chosen at random
Plucked from Purgatory
Held for a ransom.
The heartless do not care; they never did,
They are their own directors, their own critic.
The artists, the creatives, we try to create colour
In a world, on a stage, where we see no other.

Black and white and grey and brown,
Mumma, turn that frown upside down!
She cannot, for the dread has taken over,
She gave up on her script and allowed the Fools
to drag her lower.

Each role just as important as the last

Tell yourself that as you hide under your mask.
We slave away for the Directors, but who are
they?
Living lavish lifestyles where the mountains roll
and the sun is golden
If you were not born a Director, then that is your
own problem.

No stagehand to sew up the holes,
No janitor to mop up the tears.
And if you think everyone will follow your
perfect script,
My dear, you must be on quite a trip.

They will write you out of your own words
They will cast you to the side
If you are not learned enough
Do prepare for your unseen demise.

blue eyes and purple skies

Blue eyes, purple skies,
Honey, raise that roof tonight.
Blue skies, purple eyes,
Break their hearts and leave them to die.
Build armour around your heart and never bow
down
They can't get you from so high above.

Ode to My Cat

Is there anything quite as quaint as a cat?
With their little paws pittering and pattering
Trotting along the corridor when your key hits
the lock
To flock to you, to love you, it is quite flattering.
I don't mind when he scuttles up my leg to reach
the treat in my hand
With his claws penetrating my skin
Leaving little blood berries
And a task to scrub my white jeans from within.
He can scratch, he can bite me, he can break my
favourite mug
I'll still hold him tight to my chest
He can wriggle all he wants, but mama wants a
hug.

My cat howls sometimes in the deep of the night
When the house is quiet and still.
It drives my grandma crazy, I know,
But for me, he can make all the noise he wants,
There is life in every perky trill.
His little triangle ears are a source of great
entertainment
To me
Has anyone else ever laughed at their cat doing
absolutely nothing,

Just simply existing?

I've spoiled him so.
Only water from a human drinking-glass shall
do for His Highness
And only beds of goose feathers
Appetisers with meals, of course, but no
biscuits-
He cannot abide the dryness.
He'll follow me on nighttime walks
At the halfway point, he'll depart to prowl the
streets
I'll meet him on my return
His tail in the air, the tip bending slightly as he
Pitter-patters towards me
And we'll finish the journey together.

When my heart aches during trials of sunlit days
My cat lays upon my chest and purrs,
Sings a sacred song of healing
And I run my hands over his soft fur,
I know he loves me, and I him, but
He looks permanently pissed off, and I do not
wonder why-
They let me name him when I was seven
And for a reason known only by the Heavens
I named him Baby.
And everyone just went with it.

When the World Was Ours

One day my friends knocked on my door
For the first time, and asked me out to play.
I said okay, let's seize the day,
The world is ours, let's make it count.
We stole plant pots and we swam in the river
Cycled and roller-skated
Into the sunsets
We had nothing to deliver
And all this time we were getting bigger
And no one noticed.

Back then we would laugh when we got in
trouble
And the horrors on the news left us befuddled.
We focused on cartoons,
Vibrant worlds to escape to
And we'd sometimes try to escape too,
'Running away' to the park when
Small punishments were given
Then returning home knowing
All would be forgiven.

And we would make a joke of anything tough
Guaranteed solitude within all of us,
We were forever running to find each other

Because nothing else mattered.
We would knock at each other's houses
Beg petty pennies from our parents
And go to the corner shop
Feeling like grown-ups
We didn't know any better
So we couldn't wait to grow up.

We ran wild in our childhood streets
And our creativity ran with us
When we had nothing weighing us down.
Conjuring worlds within our own
Using only what we could hold with two hands
We could see the invisible, never alone
We did not understand this place
So it was kind to us at first.

White Christmas came every year
For, it seemed, forever,
We were eager to show off our precious trinkets
Not unlike proud magpies.
Then we'd ride the blanket hills of snow
Throw soft ice at each other
And at passing cars
We'd always get away before they caught us.

I never noticed time until it hit us.
A natural disaster devastating our lives

Dragging us out of our animated worlds
And now there is nowhere to hide.
One day my friends knocked on my door
For the last time, and asked me out to play
I said okay, let's seize the day
We have no idea what the future may
Grant to us, so embrace the freedom,
Soak it in like honey on a sponge
And when that last day came to an end
I was happily ignorant, so elated I could fly
I thought those days would never die.

Individual

Individual people follow one another like sheep
Single coins; just the one could make them
weep.
One-handed barter; one-worded martyr
Sings the words of freedom.

All for one and one for all,
We all know if you believe that
Then you are just some fool who will take the
fall,
Take the fall for one who would not look twice
at all.

Single flickers of candlelight
Illuminating lonely dinners.
She sighs so loud, pushes it away.
At least she will become thinner.
Lonely hearts cry out for help, as
Help is supposedly everywhere.
"You are not alone," the crowds say in unison,
Where are they now? We're supposedly a union.

One is better than zero,
That is what they all assume.
But when everybody is living as One,

It is so freeing to break away from the fumes.
I try to stand out,
But so does she, she, she, she and he,
Walking as one but thinking like many,
How the hell did hearts become so heavy?

Sheep to the slaughter
See her? He bought her.
Two shoes in a pair
Without One it won't work
Without One it won't work.
That is how we are conditioned.
But truly, I think,
For the good of the world
For the good of our souls,
And for the good of ourselves,
Devoid of individuality,
We sheeple must be partitioned.

a haiku in honour of books

this book, once a tree

selflessly helping us breathe

treat it tenderly.

breaking down again

sometimes
we go the wrong way and
get lost
deep in the darkness
and we fall
into the abyss of despair
and it's not our fault
but we need help
not to be told
'just get on with it'
that really annoys me
just a little bit.

they can't force us to take it all on
if we know we are not ready
but they still push us to bottle it up
seal it away and
burn it up
so we can make our money
and be normal again.

it's okay though
we find solitude in each other
our tortured souls bring us together
and we can cry about our pain

we can smoke it all away
we can grow together and
heal somewhat
and then we'll have the strength
to take it all on
while still holding on to
whatever got us into this mess
in the first place.

and then
when we're ready,
we'll reach out to the passing crowds
join the current
and
be free again.

www.ingramcontent.com/pod-product-compliance
Lightning Source LLC
La Vergne TN
LVHW010927200726
843509LV00013B/2116